UMBERT
THE UNBORN

A Womb With A View

Published by Circle Press

Copyright © 2003 Circle Press
Circle Media, Inc.
432 Washington Ave.
North Haven, CT 06473
(203) 230-3800

Additional copies of this book can be obtained
by calling (800) 356-9916 ext. 3809
www.ncregister.com

ISBN 0-9743661-1-0

To my loving wife, Nancy, whose devotion, patience, and encouragement helped bring Umbert to life, and to our three children Peter, Katherine and Becca.

The Urgency of Umbert

NATIONAL ⬥ CATHOLIC
REGISTER

Umbert the Unborn Makes His Debut

Meet Umbert the Unborn, the world's first pre-natal comic strip character. He's feisty, outspoken, loveable and almost ready to take on the world.

The cartoon is making its debut in the Register's Culture of Life section this issue, but its creator hopes to see it debut in faith-based and other pro-life newspapers throughout the country this summer.

Umbert is an unborn infant of yet to be determined gender who lives in his mother's womb — "his own private universe, think tank and playground," said creator Gary Cangemi, "from which he can anticipate life and the world that awaits him and ponder

See the first installment of Umbert the Unborn on Page 16.

the primordial questions that plague us all."

Cangemi, a professional cartoonist for over 20 years, has published many cartoons and columns in defense of unborn children.

Father James Paisley, pastor of St. Maria Goretti Church near Cangemi's Scranton, Pa., home, said he is proud of the cartoon it's new work.

"In an age where the unborn child is treated like a nonentity," said Father Paisley, the cartoon "has given life, meaning and humanity to 'the child within.'"

Father Paisley brought the cartoon to the attention of Scranton Bishop James Timlin,

who was also supportive of the project.

"I want to commend you for your unique approach to making people more aware of the plight of the unborn in our society," wrote the bishop in a letter to Cangemi. "Anything we can do to humanize the unborn is most welcome and you have certainly done a great service through your artistic talent and wit."

Cangemi sees the cartoon as his contribution to the pro-life movement. He hopes that its friendly but firm approach will attract more people to respect for the unborn.

"Umbert's purpose is to give life, personality and humanity to the unborn child and to change the hearts and minds of the 'born'," he said.

Father Paisley agrees — and sees an even greater potential.

He said Umbert can help "change the face of the pro-life movement as we know it."

National Catholic Register, June 6-12, 2001

I was traveling in May 2001 when I got an "urgent" message to call Tom Hoopes. I'm the publisher and editor-in-chief of the National Catholic Register. Tom is the executive editor.

"I've just got a package from a cartoonist named Gary Cangemi," he said. "It's a cartoon strip about a character called 'Umbert the Unborn.' It reads like it was made for the Register's back page. We need to start this right away, before someone else does."

I gave the go ahead without even seeing the cartoon, hoping we weren't making a mistake.

"Umbert the Unborn" was an instant success. Immediately after it began appearing in the Register, we began getting requests to reprint it (we would refer them directly to Gary, who syndicates the cartoon at an affordable price).

All the same, we worried about Umbert in the beginning. For months, we read each installment with a bit of dread. "Will Cangemi be able to keep this up? Just one character in just in one location — and a cramped one at that — can he sustain it?" But he has. In fact, far from running out of steam, the cartoon has only gotten better over the months.

We receive many letters about Umbert. Typical of them is this one:

"Our family loves the Register. Our teen-agers (ages 13, 14 and 16) frequently read various articles — after they've checked out Umbert and Baby Mugs."

And I particularly like this one, from John Materazzo of Roxbury, Massachusetts:

"The Register is a well-done effort. I especially wish to cite Gary Cangemi's 'Umbert the Unborn' as an outstanding piece of work. It's far more than cute, cuddly and lovable. Its cutting-edge theme is creative, timely and cerebral and its humor is worthy of the top echelon of cartoonists today. His strip is terrific and should be syndicated throughout the Catholic periodical world. Thank you for your decision to carry it and to Gary for his unique talent." Umbert has made the Register's enviable demographics even younger, as evidenced by the many letters we get about Umbert from children.

Most apropos is this one, from a boy in Phoenix:

"I am 9 years old and home schooled. My favorite part of the Register is 'Umbert the Unborn.' I think he is very funny. Every week I cut out the Umbert strip and glue it on construction paper. I have made my own Umbert comic book. I enjoy reading it over and over again."

But this one, from a high-school teacher, shows that Umbert can win fans of all ages, including teen-agers:

"I began to leave the Umbert cartoons on my desk in plain view of my students, hoping to spur their concern for unborn babies. These are some guys whom you would not normally expect to care about these issues. After a while, they began taking the cutouts and showing them to other students. Now, every week they ask me where their Umbert is! So, keep up the good work; you impact many lives, even those you least suspect!"

These letters show how badly needed Umbert is today. It is an upbeat, positive cartoon that carries an urgently needed message. Our culture can be deaf to the pro-life message, because it has put up barriers to common sense on the topic of abortion. But by making readers laugh, Umbert bounces happily past those barriers and delivers his message directly to the heart.

Fr Owen Kearns LC

Father Owen Kearns, LC
Publisher and Editor-in-Chief
National Catholic Register

A Star is Unborn

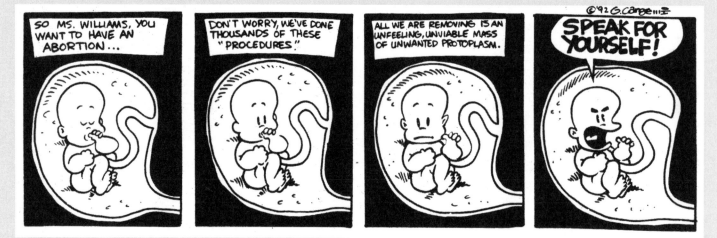

The original inspiration for *Umbert the Unborn*. From Gary Cangemi's "Off the Board" (Published in *The Metro*, 1992)

When my mom first conveyed to me the facts of life (my dad's version being somewhat vague), one thing was made abundantly clear: only women could conceive babies. Little did I realize then that 30 years later I would destroy that myth when I conceived and gave "unbirth" to the world's first syndicated pro-life, prenatal cartoon baby.

What amazes me most about "Umbert the Unborn" is how fascinated people are with how I conceived Umbert in the first place. The two most frequently asked questions I get are "How did you come up with Umbert?" and "Where did you get that name?"

The idea for Umbert began in 1992 when I drew freelance political cartoons for a Scranton, Pennsylvania, weekly newspaper. I had my own half-page called "Off the Board" on which I was given free rein to tackle any topic I wished.

Always passionate about my pro-life views, I dedicated one installment to the abortion issue. Included in the group of cartoons was a four-panel strip about a baby in the womb about to be aborted, overhearing the doctor dismissing him as an unfeeling, unviable mass of unwanted protoplasm, to which the baby replies, "SPEAK FOR YOURSELF!"

Around that same time, Helen Gohsler, president of our local pro-life chapter, asked me to come up with a creative way to present pro-life issues to children. I told her I would think about it, and, nine years later, I was still thinking about it.

In the spring of 2001, I was feeling very depressed. My mom had recently lost a six-year battle with cancer and I was feeling my career as an artist going nowhere. I felt my mother's spirit urging me to pray for God's guidance, and I did. Soon after, I was browsing through some old clippings of my work when I came upon that strip of the baby about to be aborted. As soon as I saw that defiant little tyke raising his voice in self-affirmation, a cartoon light bulb went on over my head and I knew God had answered my prayers.

Why "Umbert"? I wanted a heroic-sounding name for the title of my strip, evoking the image of a warrior-hero, fighting for a noble cause — something that sounded like "Richard the Lion-Hearted" or "Peter the Great."

"_____ the Unborn," I thought, but I wanted a name that began with the letter "U" so it would be alliterative. I spent hours on this but I couldn't think of any. Then I remembered a book I had read, *The Name of the Rose*, by Umberto Eco, but "Umberto the Unborn" sounded too ethnic. I simply dropped the extra vowel and Umbert was "unborn."

The reaction to Umbert has been, to say the least, overwhelming and extremely gratifying, especially to a small-town cartoonist whose work was rarely seen beyond the endless mountains of northeast Pennsylvania. While a few eyebrows have been raised over the notion of using humor to fight the culture of death, I believe humor can be a very powerful weapon in the cause of life. We pro-lifers can get pretty worked up over the intense and emotional issues we are fighting for and a good laugh can provide relief from the stress. I like to think of Umbert as a kind of prenatal Bob Hope, entertaining the front-line troops of the pro-life cause and giving them a much-needed morale boost.

As for Helen's request, I think Umbert is a great way to introduce children to the pro-life movement and to educate them on the moral and ethical problems with which abortion confronts us. Whole generations of Americans are being raised on the notion that infanticide is nothing more than a safe, legal medical procedure and a constitutional "right." Millions of children have paid with their lives for this egregious and erroneous misinterpretation of our founding documents.

Unlike any other form of entertainment, a cartoon character can form a unique bond with people of all ages. Umbert was created to give a face and a voice to the unborn child, to urge us to see the unborn child as a real person with yet-unfulfilled dreams and expectations. Umbert is "Everybaby" in his own four-panel morality play. If Umbert can succeed in making his death at the hands of an abortionist unthinkable, then he will have accomplished his life's work — before being born!

On that note, a young boy from Kentucky asked me when Umbert would finally be born. I told him that the day when the natural right of all children to be born was guaranteed in law — that will be Umbert's birthday. It's a promise I hope and pray to be able to keep in my lifetime.

Until that day, Umbert is scheduled for a very long stay in his mother's womb, but that's okay. Umbert gets plenty of "womb service," loves to read his Unborn Times, and has lots of time to answer his "pre-mail" on the "Interwomb."

As Umbert would say ... "Imagination. God's a genius!"

Your Friend for "Life,"

Gary Cangemi

Out of the Mouths of Unborn Babes

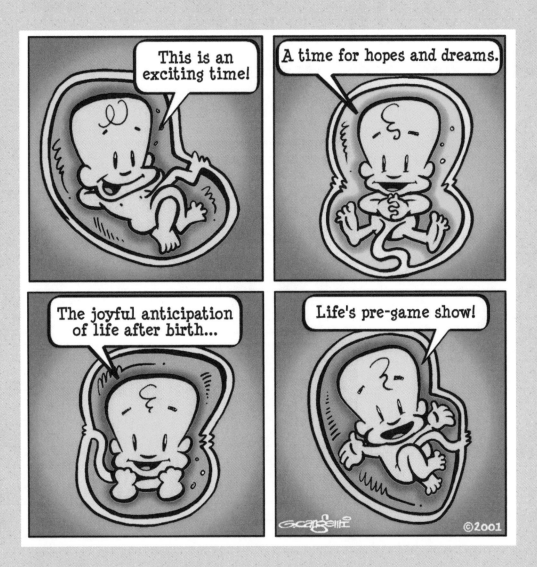

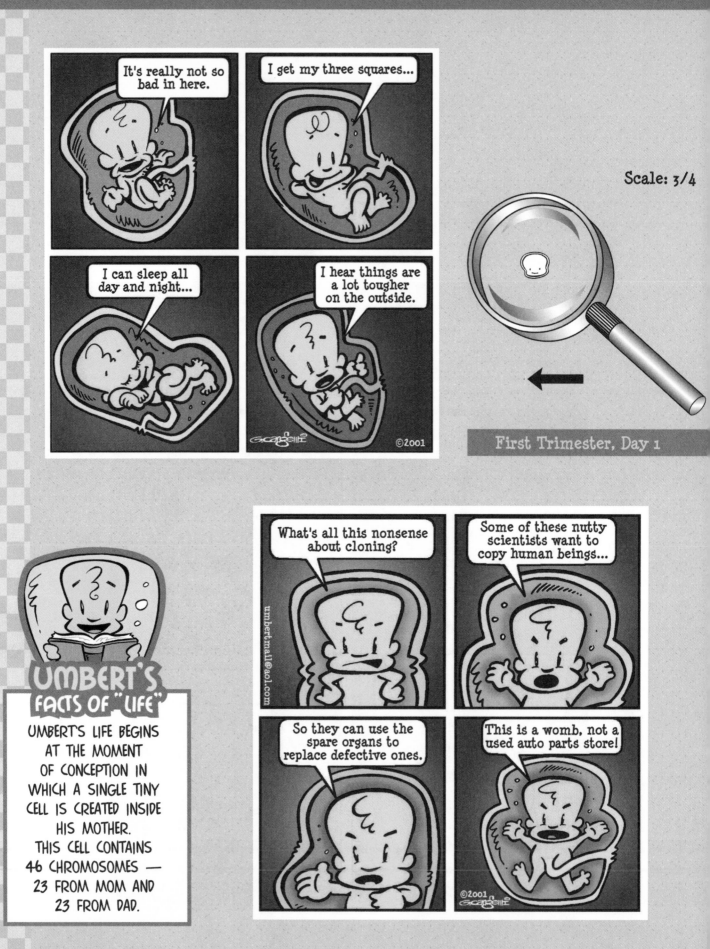

Scale: 3/4

First Trimester, Day 1

UMBERT'S FACTS OF "LIFE"

UMBERT'S LIFE BEGINS AT THE MOMENT OF CONCEPTION IN WHICH A SINGLE TINY CELL IS CREATED INSIDE HIS MOTHER. THIS CELL CONTAINS 46 CHROMOSOMES — 23 FROM MOM AND 23 FROM DAD.

UMBERT'S FACTS OF "LIFE"

UMBERT'S 46 CHROMOSOMES DETERMINE UMBERT'S "GENOTYPE," A BLUEPRINT OF UMBERT'S INHERITED TRAITS SUCH AS EYE AND HAIR COLOR, SKIN TONE, FACIAL FEATURES AND GENDER.

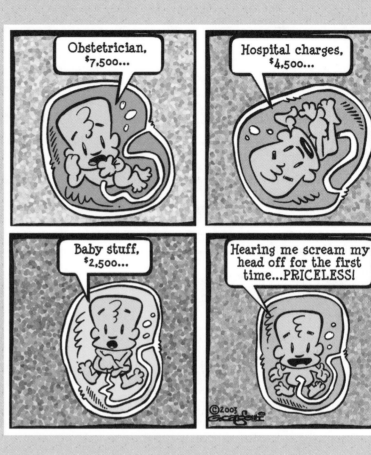

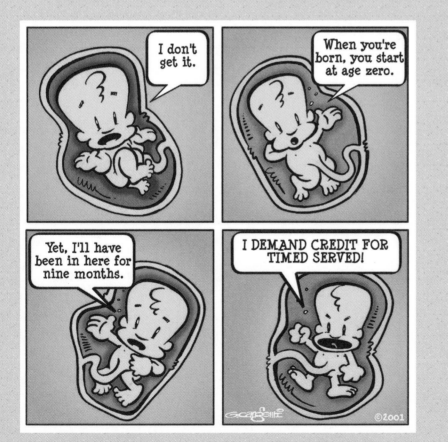

First Trimester, Day 4

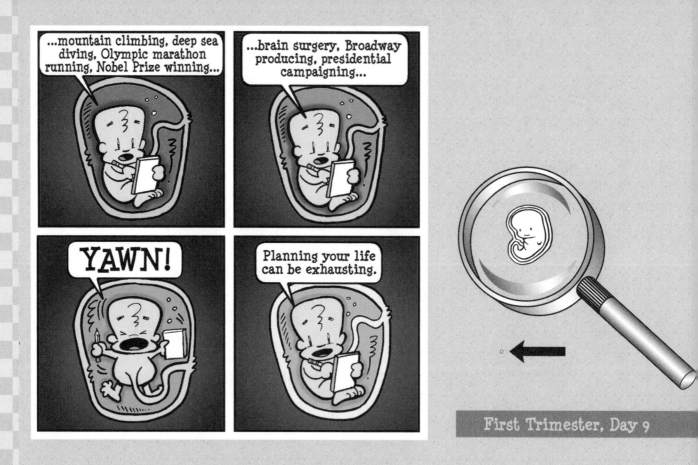

First Trimester, Day 9

UMBERT'S FACTS OF "LIFE"

IN JUST 7 TO 9 DAYS AFTER FERTILIZATION, UMBERT HAS GROWN TO ABOUT A HUNDRED CELLS IN SIZE.

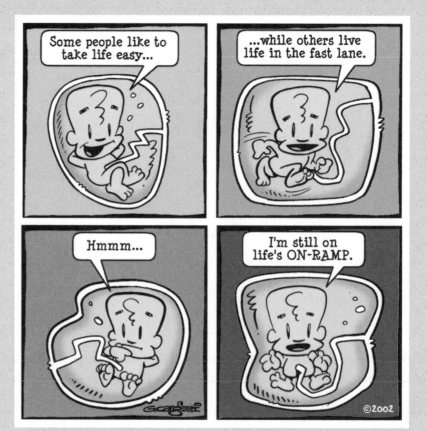

UMBERT'S FACTS OF "LIFE"

UMBERT'S HEART FORMS IN AS EARLY AS 18 DAYS AND BEGINS BEATING ON ABOUT DAY 24.

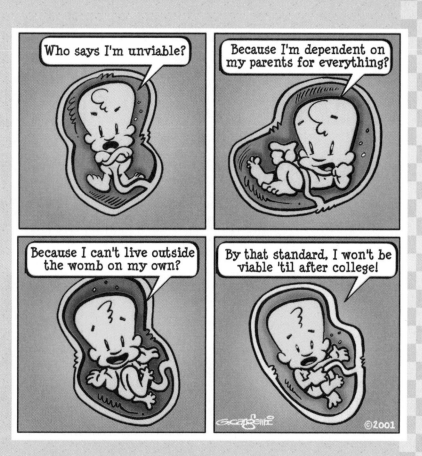

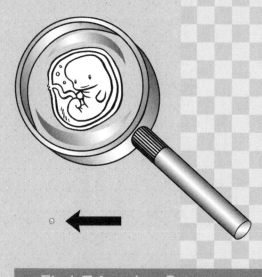

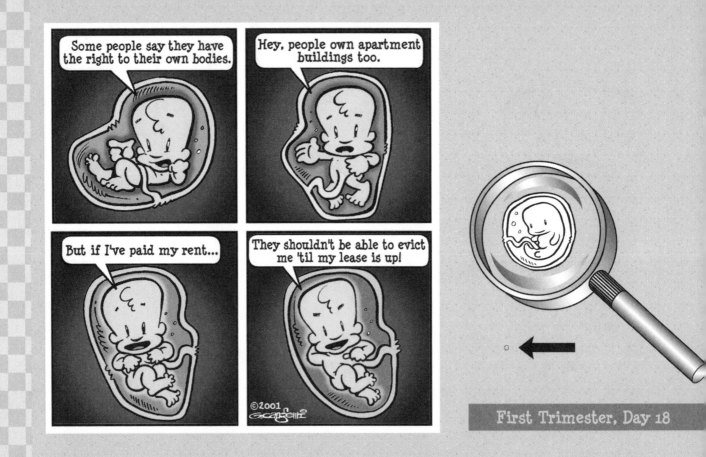

First Trimester, Day 18

UMBERT'S FACTS OF "LIFE"

BY THE 20TH DAY, UMBERT'S BRAIN, SPINE AND NERVOUS SYSTEM HAVE BEGUN TO DEVELOP.

UMBERT'S FACTS OF "LIFE"

WHAT DOES UMBERT DO FOR FUN? AT FOUR MONTHS GESTATION, HE CAN DO SOMERSAULTS IN THE WOMB.

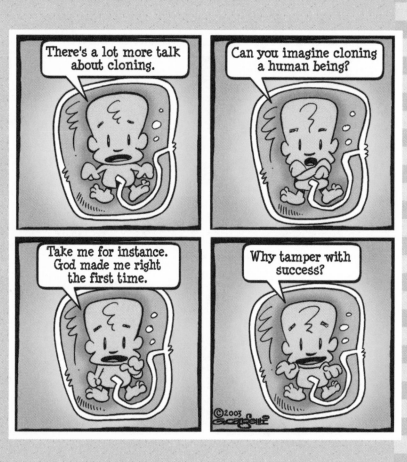

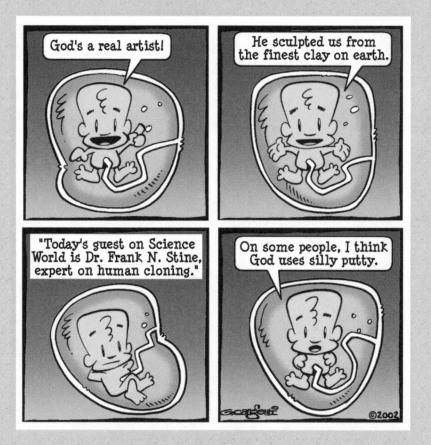

First Trimester, Day 24

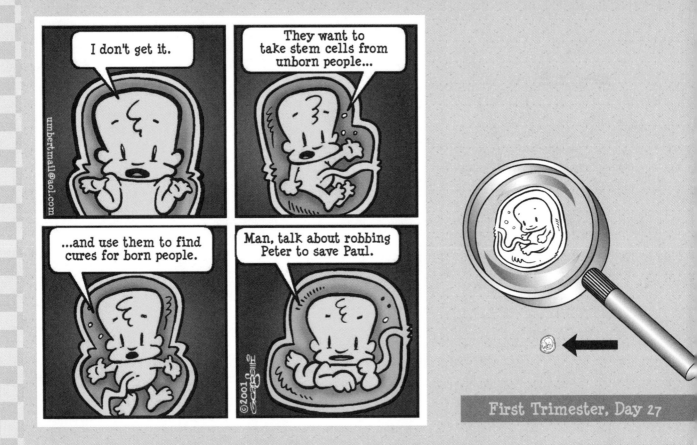

First Trimester, Day 27

UMBERT'S FACTS OF "LIFE"

AT 43 DAYS AFTER CONCEPTION, IT IS POSSIBLE TO RECORD UMBERT'S BRAIN WAVES.

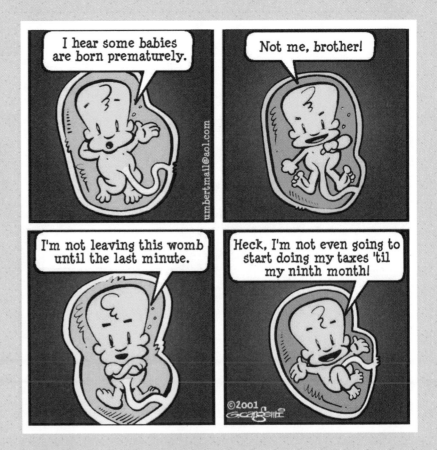

Pro-Life Umbert

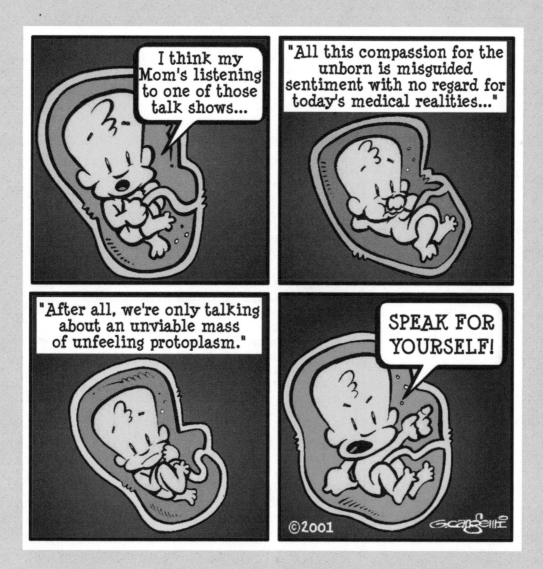

First Trimester, Day 31

UMBERT'S FACTS OF "LIFE"

AT EIGHT AND A HALF WEEKS, UMBERT'S FINGERPRINTS ARE FORMED.

UMBERT'S FACTS OF "LIFE"

A BIG HAND FOR UMBERT. AT 11 WEEKS, UMBERT CAN FIT INTO THE PALM OF HIS DAD'S HAND.

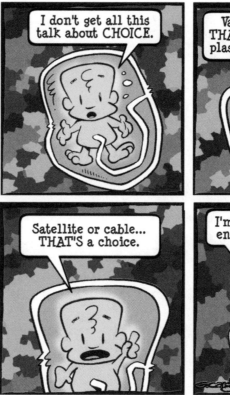

I don't get all this talk about CHOICE.

Vanilla or chocolate... THAT'S a choice. Paper or plastic...THAT'S a choice.

Satellite or cable... THAT'S a choice.

I'm a child, not a home entertainment system!

©2003

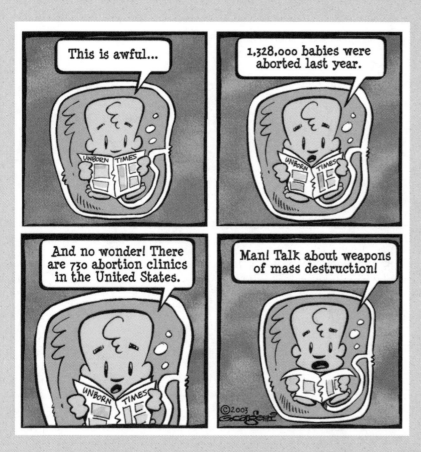

This is awful...

1,328,000 babies were aborted last year.

And no wonder! There are 730 abortion clinics in the United States.

Man! Talk about weapons of mass destruction!

©2003

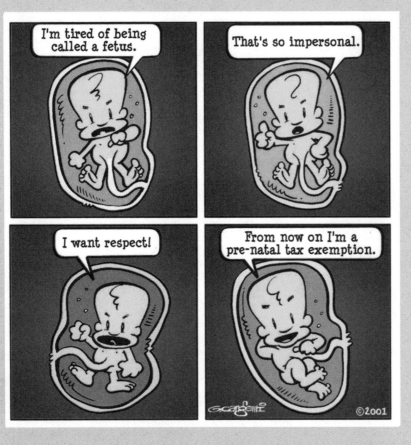

First Trimester, Day 40

UMBERT'S FACTS OF "LIFE"

IN BUFFALO, NY, A 2 POUND BABY GIRL WAS DELIVERED ONE WEEK AFTER HER MOTHER WAS PRONOUNCED BRAIN DEAD. HER MOTHER WAS ON LIFE SUPPORT TO INCREASE THE CHILD'S CHANCE OF SURVIVAL.

(AMA JOURNAL, SEPT. 1982)

UMBERT'S FACTS OF "LIFE"

USING ULTRASOUND, DOCTORS DIAGNOSED AN UNBORN CHILD'S HEART BEATING AT 260 BEATS PER MINUTE. AFTER MEDICATING THE MOTHER, THE FETAL HEART RATE DROPPED TO 125-130 BEATS PER MINUTE WITHIN AN HOUR.

(NEW ENGLAND JOURNAL OF MEDICINE, JUNE 1981)

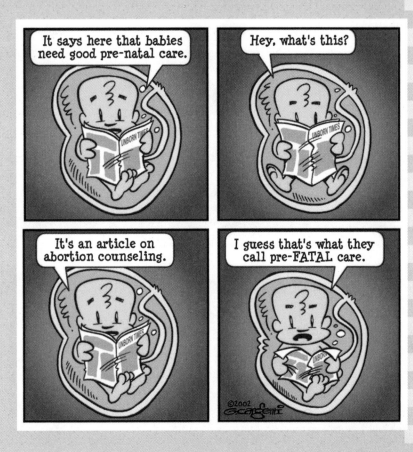

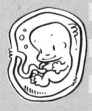

First Trimester, Day 50

UMBERT'S FACTS OF "LIFE"

SURGERY CAN NOW BE PERFORMED ON UNBORN CHILDREN IN THE WOMB. ONE TINY PATIENT ACTUALLY REACHED OUT AND GRASPED THE DOCTOR'S FINGER.

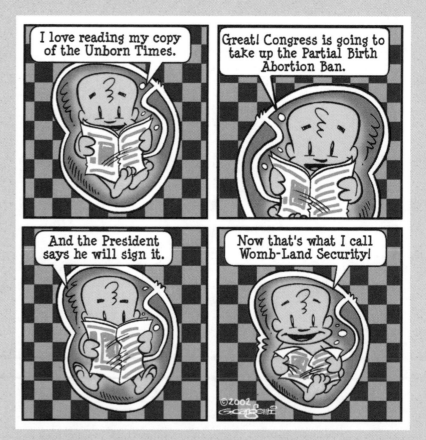

UMBERT'S FACTS OF "LIFE"

WHEN WILL UMBERT BE BORN? THAT'S UP TO UMBERT. NORMALLY, THE BABY DETERMINES THE DURATION OF THE PREGNANCY.

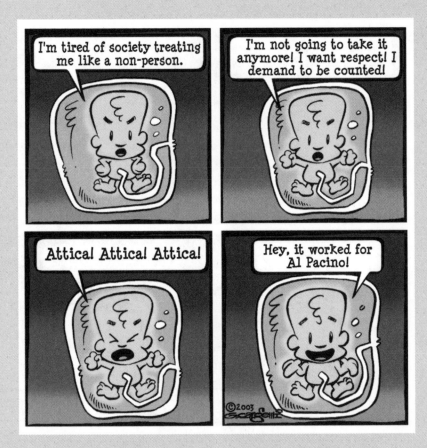

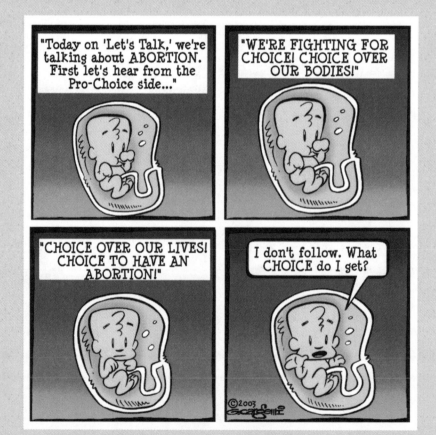

First Trimester, Day 59

UMBERT'S FACTS OF "LIFE"

IN THE EIGHTH MONTH, UMBERT CAN ACTUALLY HEAR SOUNDS FROM THE OUTSIDE WORLD AND CAN BE STARTLED BY SUDDEN NOISES.

God's a Genius!

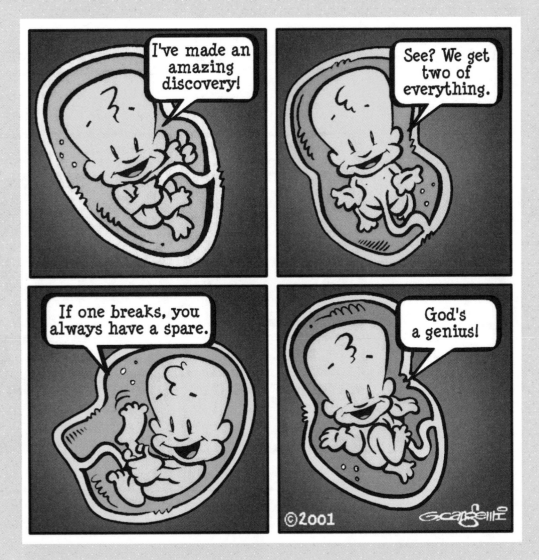

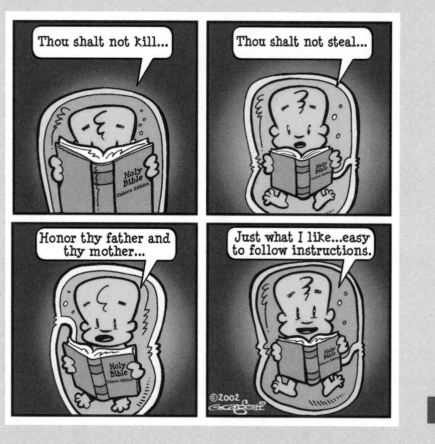

First Trimester, Day 65

UMBERT'S FACTS OF "LIFE"

AT 8 WEEKS, UMBERT'S HEART CAN BE HEARD BEATING USING AN ULTRASONIC STETHOSCOPE.

UMBERT'S FACTS OF "LIFE"

CLASSICAL MUSIC CAN KEEP UMBERT CALM IN THE WOMB. JUST DON'T PLAY THE CANON-HEAVY 1812 OVERTURE!

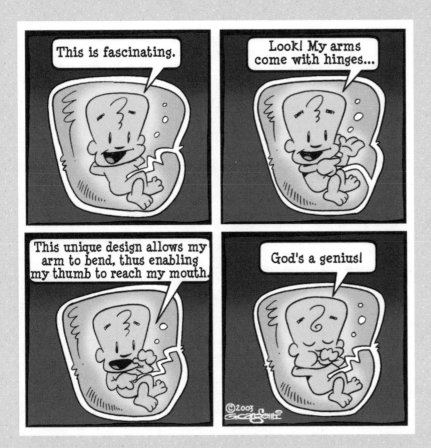

First Trimester, Day 75

UMBERT'S FACTS OF "LIFE"

HALFWAY THROUGH MOM'S PREGNANCY, UMBERT IS A FOOT LONG AND WEIGHS ABOUT A POUND.

UMBERT'S FACTS OF "LIFE"

IN 17 DAYS, UMBERT'S FIRST BLOOD CELLS ARE FORMED.

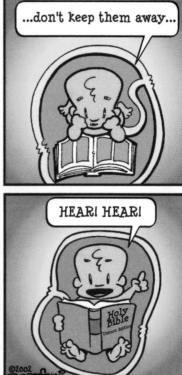

First Trimester, Day 80

First Trimester, Day 87

UMBERT'S
FACTS OF "LIFE"

EMPEROR VALENTINIAN
DECREED IN 374 A.D. THAT
ALL PARENTS MUST
SUPPORT THEIR CONCEIVED
CHILDREN.

Umbert's Family

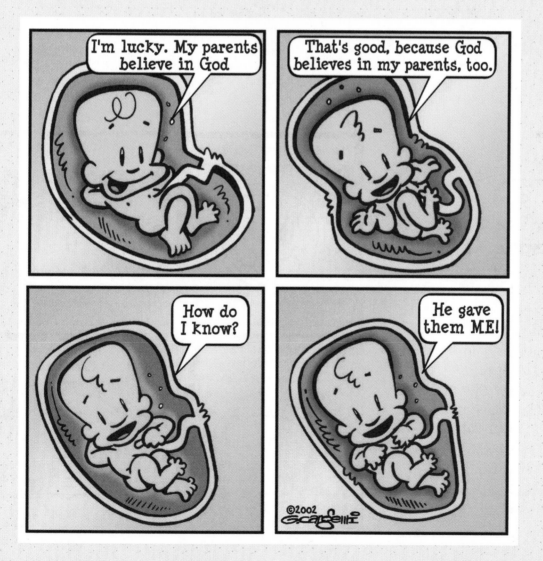

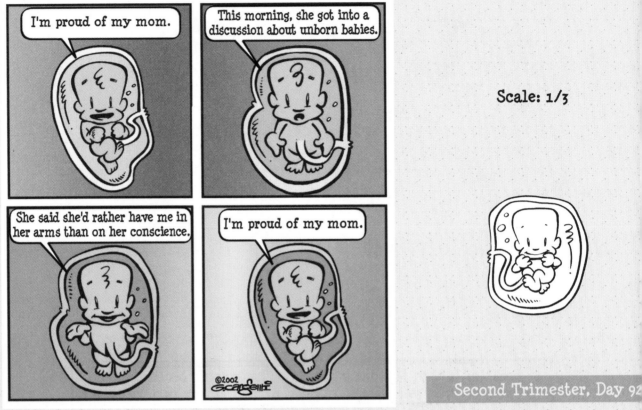

Scale: 1/3

Second Trimester, Day 92

UMBERT'S FACTS OF "LIFE"

WOMEN WHO GO TO CRISIS PREGNANCY CENTERS USUALLY SEEK AN ABORTION. ONCE FULLY INFORMED, ABOUT 80% CHANGE THEIR MINDS AND CHOOSE LIFE.

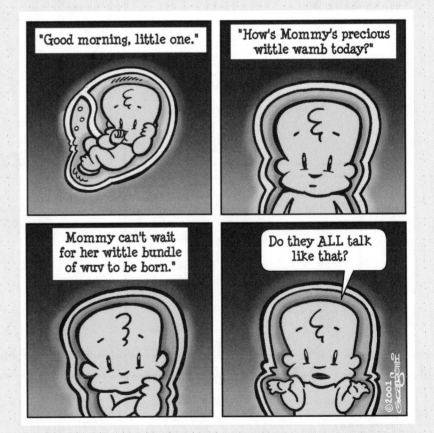

UMBERT'S FACTS OF "LIFE"

AT SEVEN WEEKS, UMBERT ALREADY LOOKS LIKE A MINIATURE BABY COMPLETE WITH ARMS, LEGS, FINGERS AND TOES, BUT IS ONLY ONE INCH LONG.

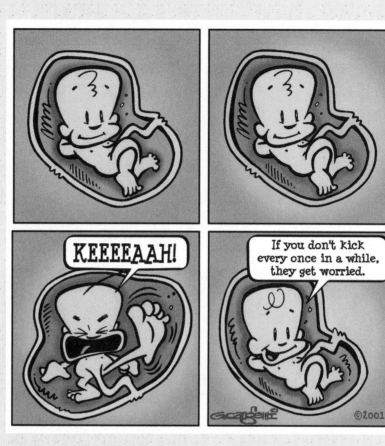

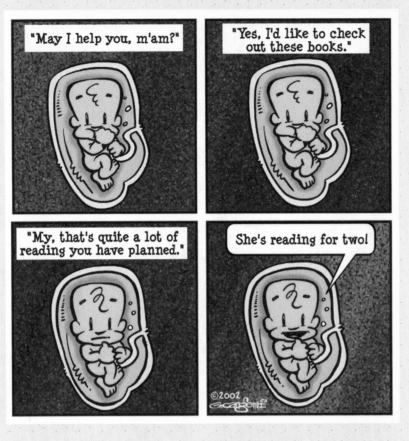

Second Trimester, Day 1

UMBERT'S FACTS OF "LIFE"

BY 14 WEEKS, UMBERT HAS THE SENSE OF TASTE AND CAN SWALLOW.

UMBERT'S FACTS OF "LIFE"

IRELAND PASSED THE WORLD'S FIRST CONSTITUTIONAL AMENDMENT PROTECTING THE UNBORN FROM CONCEPTION.

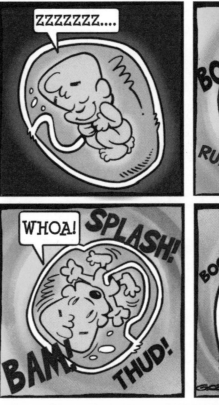

Second Trimester, Day 1c

UMBERT'S FACTS OF "LIFE"

TO PROTECT INNOCENT HUMAN LIFE, "GOOD" KING WENCESLAS OUTLAWED CHILD ABANDONMENT AND CRIMINALIZED ABORTION.

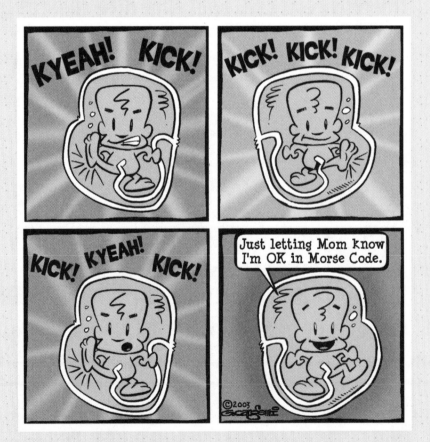

UMBERT'S FACTS OF "LIFE"

IN THE EARLY DAYS OF OUR NATION, LAWS PROTECTED THE UNBORN CHILD AT "QUICKENING," THE TIME WHEN THE MOTHER FIRST FELT LIFE STIRRING WITHIN HER.

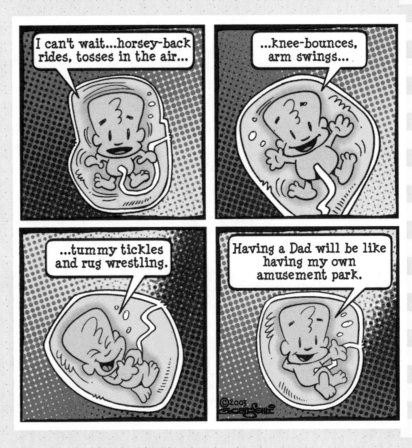

Second Trimester, Day 114

Second Trimester, Day 12

UMBERT'S FACTS OF "LIFE"

IN THE 19TH CENTURY, THE ANTI-ABORTION MOVEMENT WAS LED BY THE AMERICAN MEDICAL ASSOCIATION.

UMBERT'S FACTS OF "LIFE"

THE PRO-LIFE MOVEMENT IS THE LARGEST "GRASS ROOTS" EFFORT IN THE HISTORY OF THE UNITED STATES.

Uh-oh!

Puff!Puff!Puff! Puff!Puff!Puff!

There it goes again.

Either a steam locomotive just went by...

...or Mom's doing her LaMaze again.

©2001

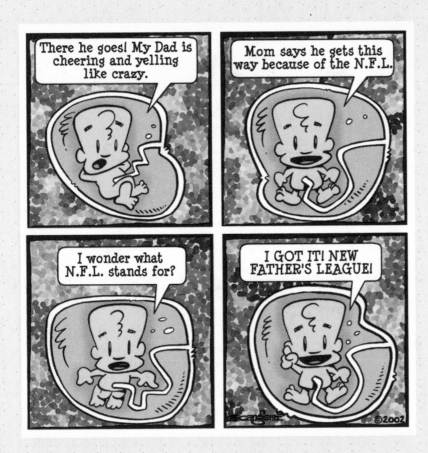

There he goes! My Dad is cheering and yelling like crazy.

Mom says he gets this way because of the N.F.L.

I wonder what N.F.L. stands for?

I GOT IT! NEW FATHER'S LEAGUE!

©2002

Second Trimester, Day 125

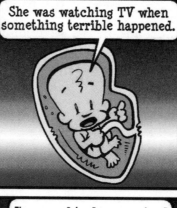

UMBERT'S FACTS OF "LIFE"

BY THE END OF THE FIRST TRIMESTER, UMBERT IS "BREATHING" AMNIOTIC FLUID AND CONTINUES TO DO SO UNTIL BIRTH.

UMBERT'S FACTS OF "LIFE"

SAINT IGNATIUS LOYOLA CALLED ABORTION A MURDEROUS ACT, AN AWFUL TYRANNY AND A SMEAR AGAINST GOD.

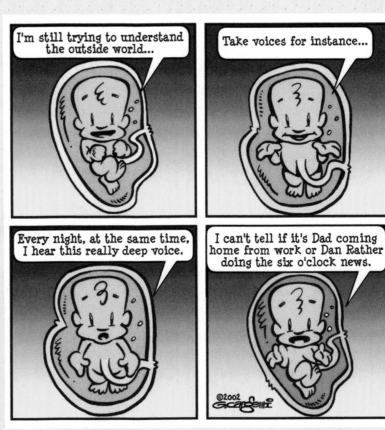

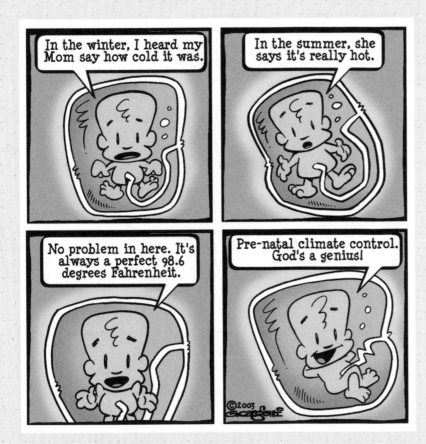

Second Trimester, Day 134

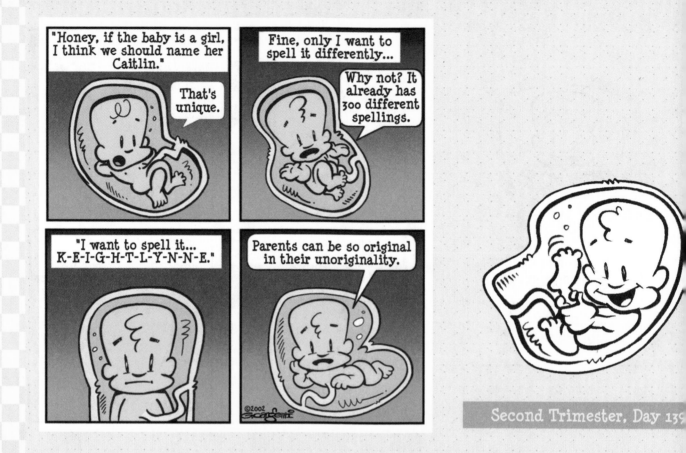

Second Trimester, Day 139

UMBERT'S FACTS OF "LIFE"

FAMED SUFFRAGETTE SUSAN B. ANTHONY WAS VEHEMENTLY OPPOSED TO ABORTION AND LINKED IT TO THE EXPLOITATION OF WOMEN.

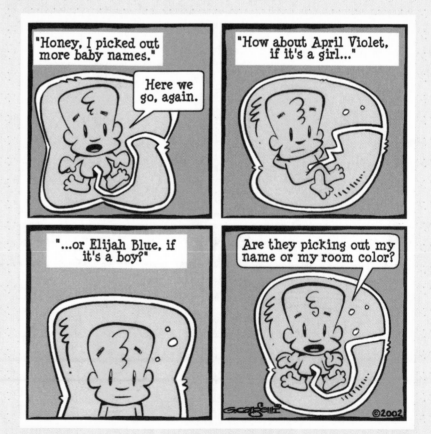

Umbert the Embryo

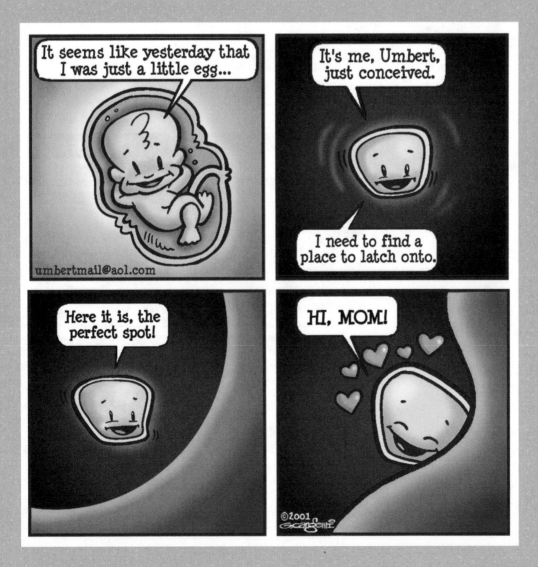

Second Trimester, Day 14

UMBERT'S
FACTS OF "LIFE"

LEGALIZED ABORTION HAS
KILLED MORE AMERICANS
THAN ALL OF ITS WARS
COMBINED.

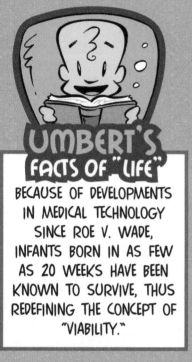

UMBERT'S FACTS OF "LIFE"

BECAUSE OF DEVELOPMENTS IN MEDICAL TECHNOLOGY SINCE ROE V. WADE, INFANTS BORN IN AS FEW AS 20 WEEKS HAVE BEEN KNOWN TO SURVIVE, THUS REDEFINING THE CONCEPT OF "VIABILITY."

Second Trimester, Day 150

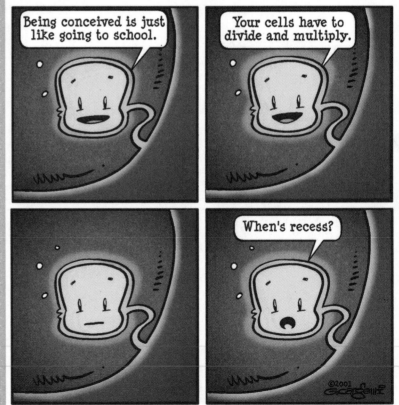

umbertmail@aol.com

UMBERT'S FACTS OF "LIFE"

SOME 43 MILLION AMERICAN CHILDREN HAVE LOST THEIR LIVES DUE TO "LEGAL" ABORTIONS.

What's with some of these politicians?

They say I'm not a human being until I latch onto my mother's womb.

LATCH!

OK, I give up. What's the difference?

©2002

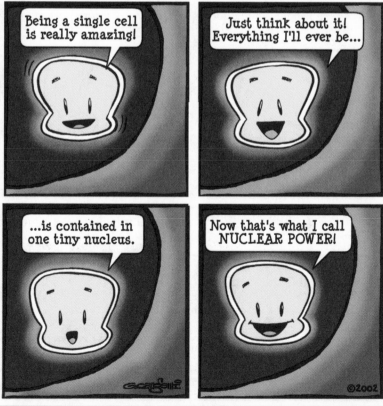

Being a single cell is really amazing!

Just think about it! Everything I'll ever be...

...is contained in one tiny nucleus.

Now that's what I call NUCLEAR POWER!

©2002

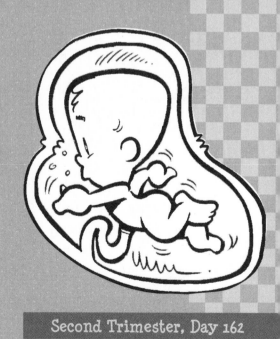

Second Trimester, Day 162

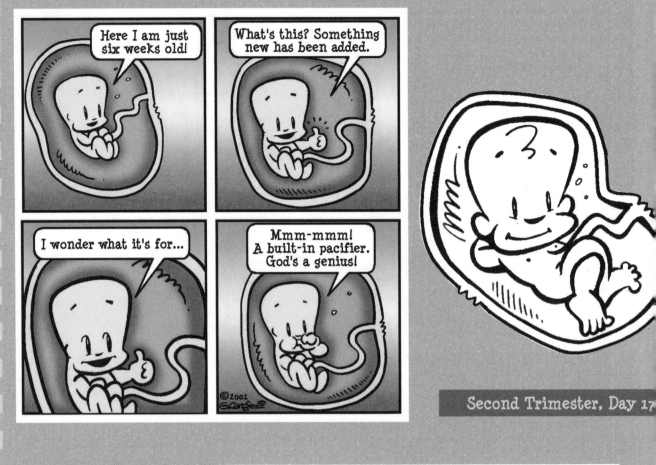

Second Trimester, Day 17

UMBERT'S FACTS OF "LIFE"

UMBERT GETS A STEADY SUPPLY OF OXYGEN FROM HIS UMBILICAL CORD UNTIL THE LUNGS TAKE OVER AT BIRTH.

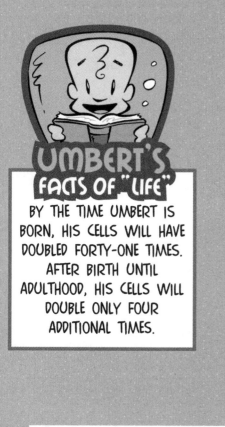

UMBERT'S FACTS OF "LIFE"

BY THE TIME UMBERT IS BORN, HIS CELLS WILL HAVE DOUBLED FORTY-ONE TIMES. AFTER BIRTH UNTIL ADULTHOOD, HIS CELLS WILL DOUBLE ONLY FOUR ADDITIONAL TIMES.

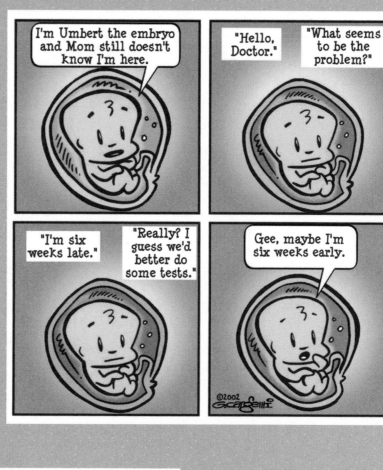

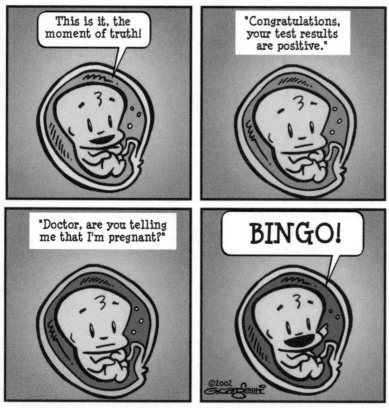

Second Trimester, Day 175

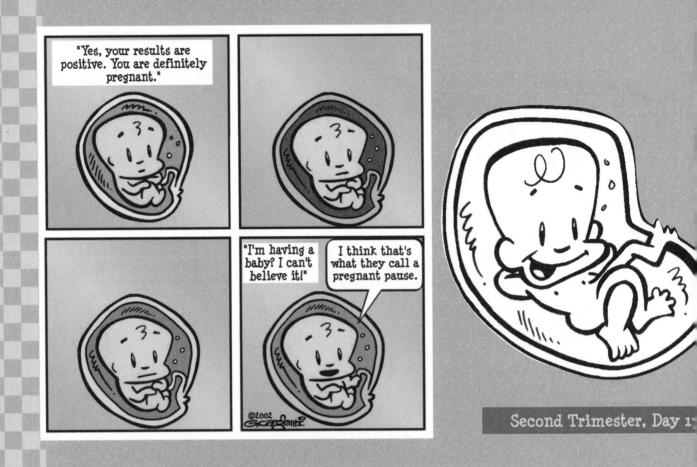

Second Trimester, Day 1-

UMBERT'S FACTS OF "LIFE"

AT ABOUT ONE WEEK AFTER CONCEPTION, UMBERT PLANTS HIMSELF IN THE NUTRITIONAL LINING OF HIS MOTHER'S UTERUS. HIS BODY CONTAINS ABOUT 256 CELLS.

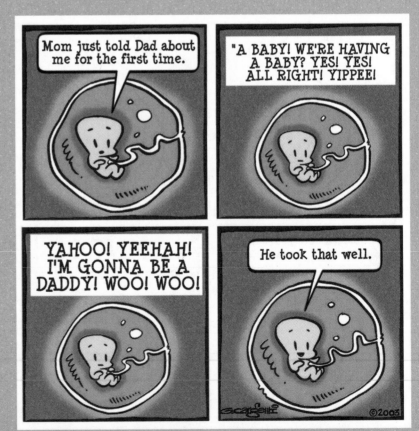

Womb Mates

Scale: 1/6

Third Trimester, Day 185

UMBERT'S FACTS OF "LIFE"

FRATERNAL (NON-IDENTICAL) TWINS ARE CREATED WHEN TWO EGGS ARE FERTILIZED SEPARATELY DURING THE SAME CYCLE. IDENTICAL TWINS ARE FORMED WHEN ONE FERTILIZED EGG DIVIDES AND THE TWO HALVES GROW INDEPENDENTLY, CREATING TWO DISTINCT HUMAN BEINGS.

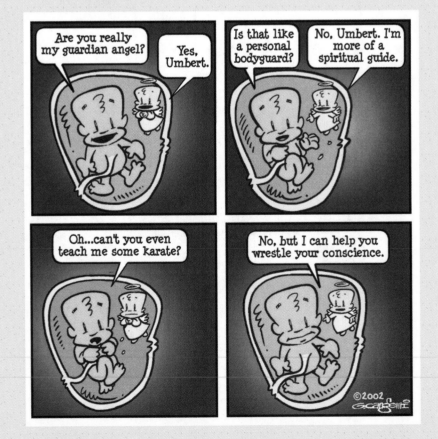

UMBERT'S FACTS OF "LIFE"

"PHYSICIANS, BIOLOGISTS AND OTHER SCIENTISTS AGREE THAT CONCEPTION MARKS THE BEGINNING OF THE LIFE OF A HUMAN BEING - A BEING THAT IS ALIVE AND IS A MEMBER OF THE HUMAN SPECIES."

(SENATE REPORT, 97TH CONGRESS, S-158)

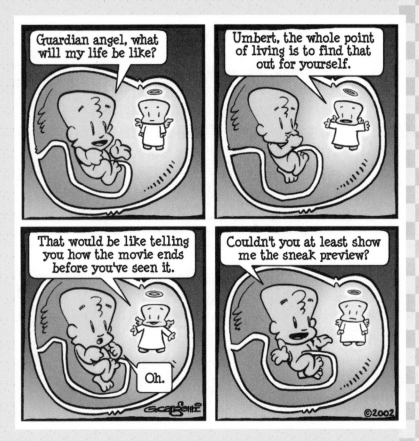

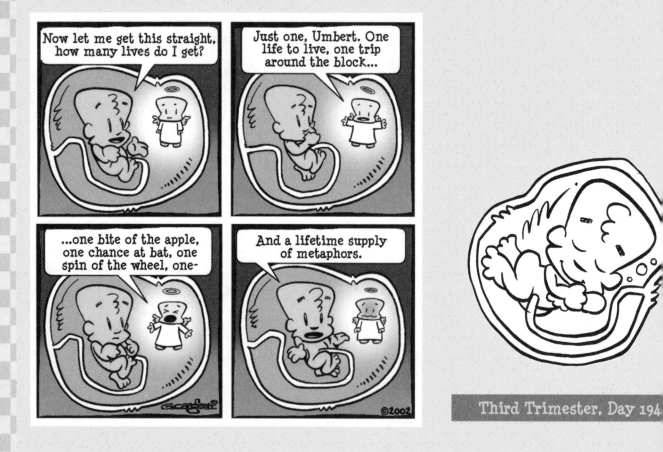

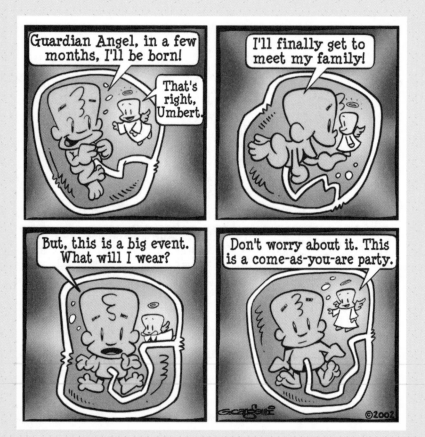

Third Trimester, Day 194

UMBERT'S FACTS OF "LIFE"

UMBERT IS A "ZYGOTE" OR FERTILIZED EGG WHEN CONCEIVED. ONCE HIS CELLS BEGIN TO DIVIDE HE BECOMES AN "EMBRYO."

UMBERT'S FACTS OF "LIFE"

AS EARLY AS FORTY DAYS, UMBERT'S BRAIN WAVES CAN BE RECORDED.

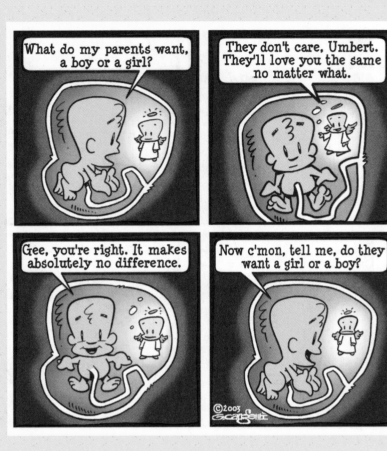

Third Trimester, Day 198

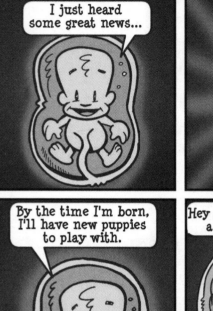

Third Trimester, Day 204

UMBERT'S FACTS OF "LIFE"

UMBERT'S EIGHT SECONDS OF FAME ... A NEW CHILD IS BORN IN THE UNITED STATES EVERY 8 SECONDS.

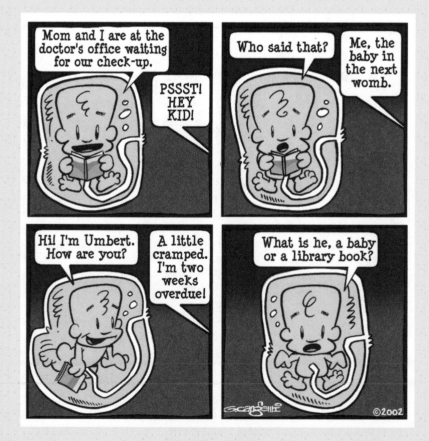

'Tis the Season to be Umbert

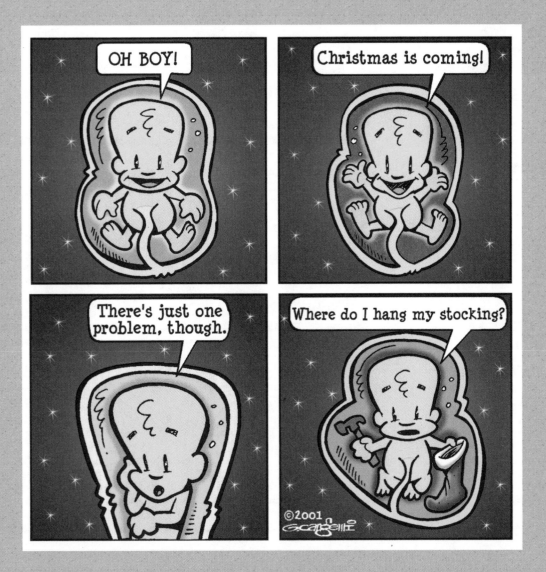

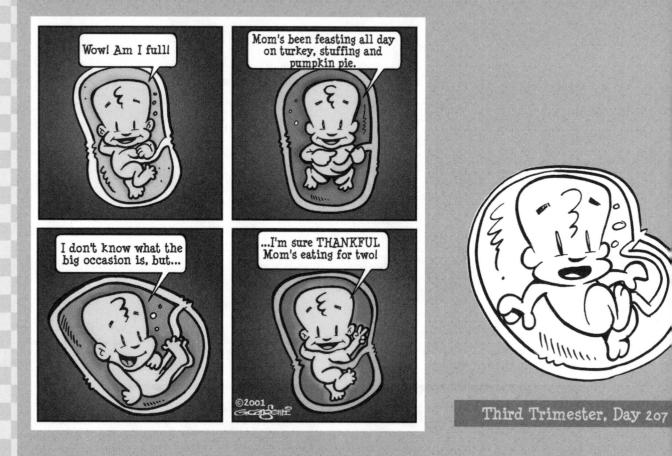

Third Trimester, Day 207

UMBERT'S FACTS OF "LIFE"

AT 12 WEEKS, UMBERT CAN ACTUALLY "SWIM" IN THE AMNIOTIC FLUID WHICH SURROUNDS HIM.

UMBERT'S FACTS OF "LIFE"

BY 16 WEEKS, UMBERT HAS EYELASHES AND FINE HAIR ON HIS HEAD.

Jesus was one lucky baby.

When he was born he had shepherds, angels, kings and everything.

And best of all, two loving parents!

Now that's what I call a Merry Christmas!

©2002

Wow! Jesus was once an unborn baby like me.

But on the way to Bethlehem, his Mom had to carry him while riding on the back of a donkey.

That must have been one bumpy ride.

I get bounced around when Mom drives the S.U.V.

©2001

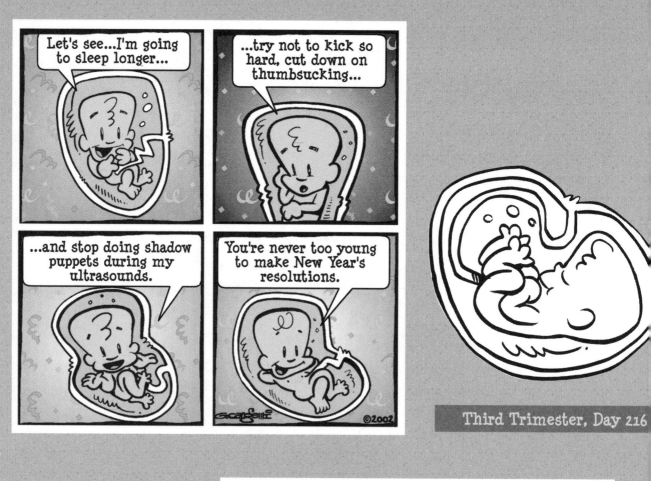

Third Trimester, Day 216

UMBERT'S FACTS OF "LIFE"

IF UMBERT HAS AN ITCH, HE HAS TO WAIT ABOUT 20 WEEKS TO SCRATCH IT. THAT'S WHEN HIS FINGERNAILS ARE FORMED.

UMBERT'S FACTS OF "LIFE"

BY THE END OF THE SECOND TRIMESTER, UMBERT HAS FULLY DEVELOPED VOCAL CORDS. MOM CAN'T HEAR HER BABY CRY THOUGH, BECAUSE HE'S STILL UNDER WATER.

I love a book with a happy ending!

A warm place to grow...

Wholesome, nourishing food...

And lots of T.L.C.

Moms, you gotta love 'em!

Happy Mothers Day

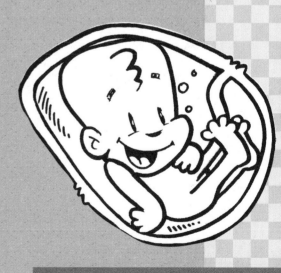

Third Trimester, Day 224

Third Trimester, Day 229

UMBERT'S FACTS OF "LIFE"

BY THE ONSET OF THE THIRD TRIMESTER, UMBERT'S BRAIN IS DEVELOPING QUICKLY AND IS CAPABLE OF LEARNING THINGS.

Where No Baby Has Gone Before

scale 1/6

Third Trimester, Day 232

UMBERT'S FACTS OF "LIFE"

THE SCI-FI FILM CLASSIC "2001: A SPACE ODYSSEY" ENDS WITH AN UNBORN CHILD SMILING DOWN AT THE PLANET EARTH.

UMBERT'S FACTS OF "LIFE"

ONE OF THE EARLY PRO-LIFERS WAS SAINT BASIL THE GREAT (FOURTH CENTURY) OF CAESAREA, WHO PREACHED THE SANCTITY OF HUMAN LIFE, OPPOSED ABORTION AND ORGANIZED FOLLOWERS TO HELP PREGNANT WOMEN.

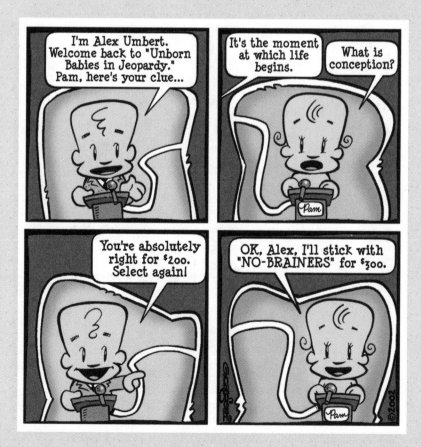

Third Trimester, Day 237

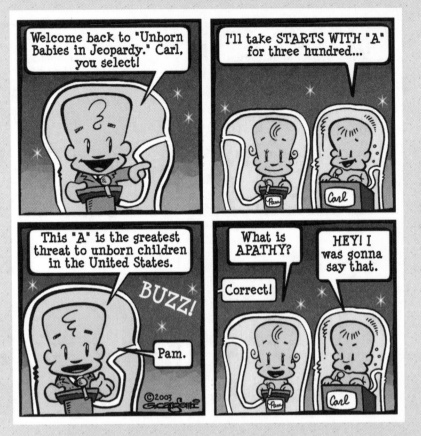

Third Trimester, Day 24[...]

UMBERT'S FACTS OF "LIFE"

BY SEVEN MONTHS, UMBERT CAN RECOGNIZE HIS MOTHER'S VOICE AND DISTINGUISH IT FROM OTHER VOICES.

UMBERT'S FACTS OF "LIFE"

WHILE IN THE WOMB, UMBERT CAN GET THE HICCUPS AND MOM CAN FEEL THEM.

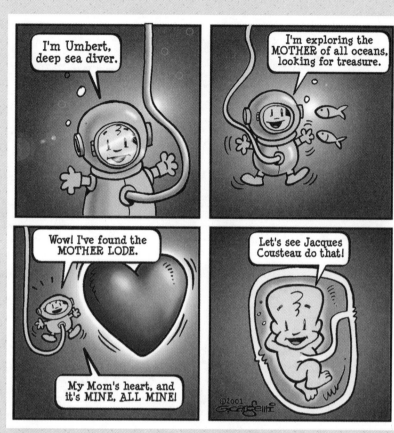

I'm Umbert, deep sea diver.

I'm exploring the MOTHER of all oceans, looking for treasure.

Wow! I've found the MOTHER LODE.

My Mom's heart, and it's MINE, ALL MINE!

Let's see Jacques Cousteau do that!

©2001

"How's the baby today, dear?"

"Very active. The baby's been kicking up a storm."

"It feels like a football game going on in there."

Just wait. Next week I'm taking up ice hockey.

©2001

Third Trimester, Day 243

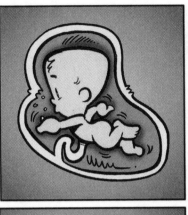
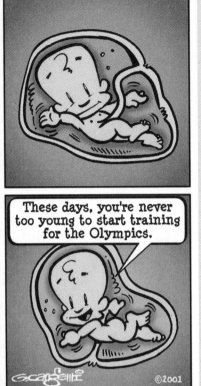
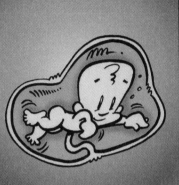

These days, you're never too young to start training for the Olympics.

©2001

Third Trimester, Day 247

UMBERT'S FACTS OF "LIFE"

BY EIGHT MONTHS, UMBERT CAN TELL THE DIFFERENCE BETWEEN LIGHT AND DARKNESS THROUGH HIS MOTHER'S ABDOMEN.

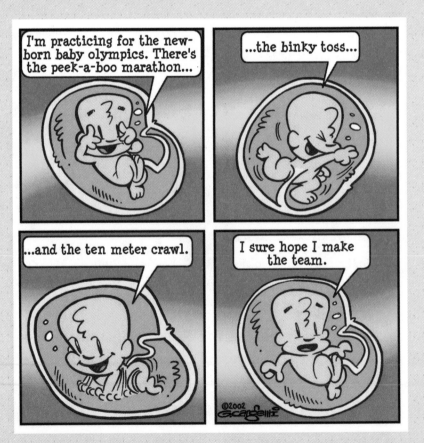

I'm practicing for the newborn baby olympics. There's the peek-a-boo marathon...

...the binky toss...

...and the ten meter crawl.

I sure hope I make the team.

©2002

Womb Service

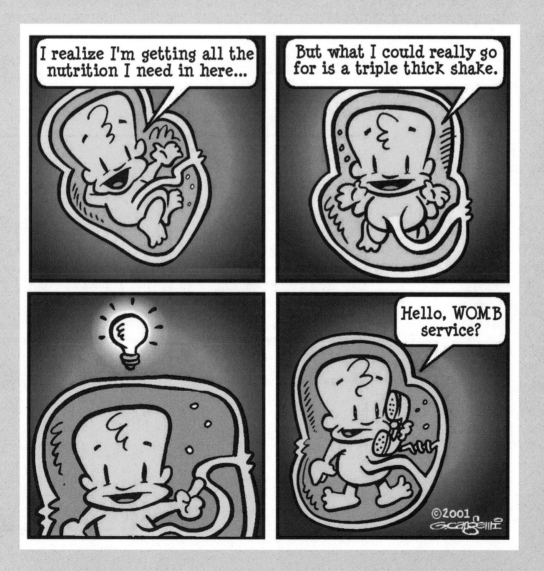

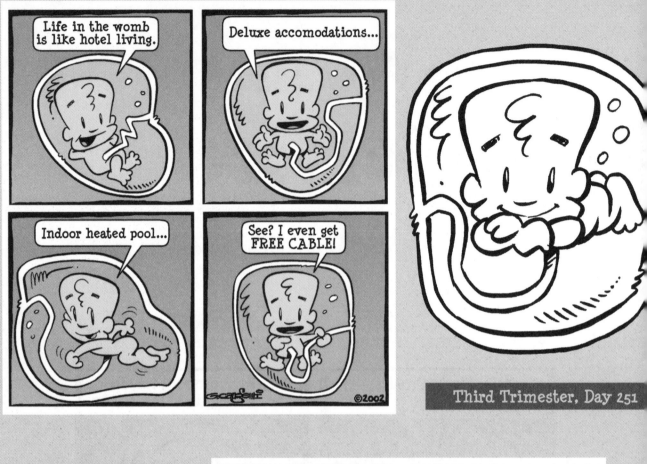

Third Trimester, Day 251

UMBERT'S FACTS OF "LIFE"

BY 32 WEEKS, UMBERT'S MOUTH IS PRETTY BUSY. HE CAN YAWN, SMILE, FROWN AND SUCK HIS THUMB ... JUST ABOUT EVERYTHING BUT HOST HIS OWN RADIO TALK SHOW.

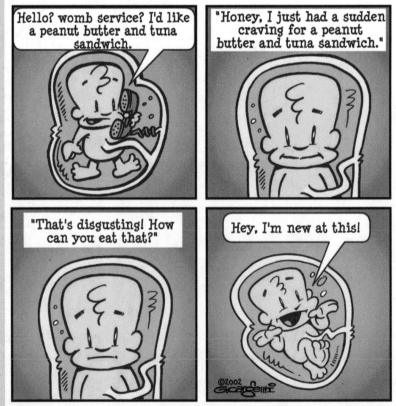

UMBERT'S FACTS OF "LIFE"

HOW MUCH WILL UMBERT WEIGH WHEN HE'S BORN? IF HE'S AVERAGE, THAT WILL BE BETWEEN 7 AND 8 POUNDS.

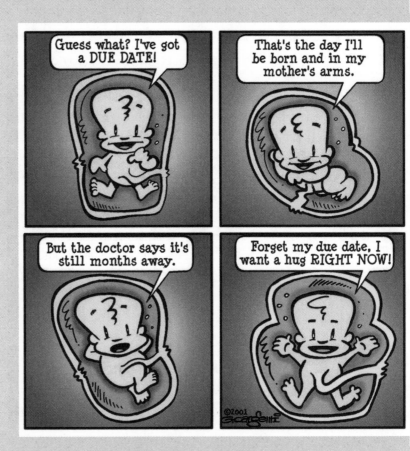

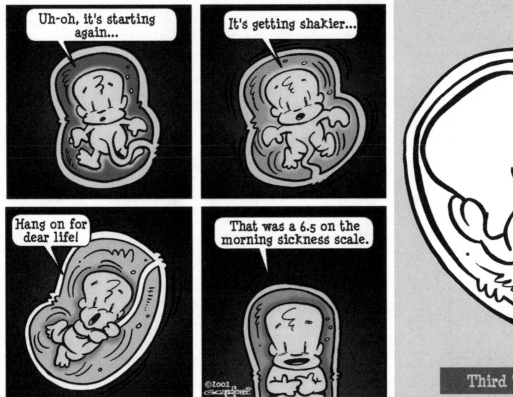

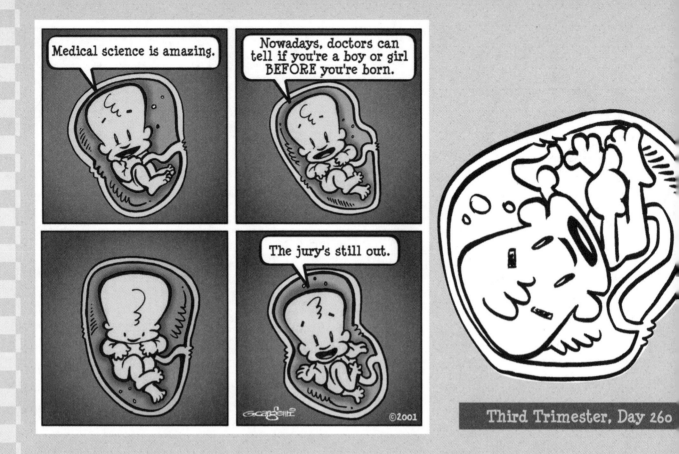

Third Trimester, Day 260

UMBERT'S FACTS OF "LIFE"

ACTOR MEL GIBSON BELIEVES, "GOD IS THE ONLY ONE WHO KNOWS HOW MANY CHILDREN WE SHOULD HAVE, AND WE SHOULD BE READY TO ACCEPT THEM."

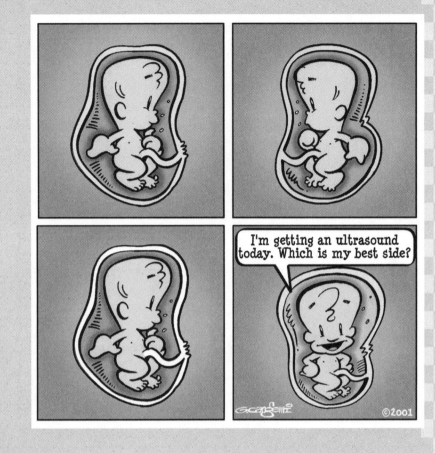

UMBERT'S FACTS OF "LIFE"

AT THE TIME OF THE ROE V. WADE DECISION, A MAJORITY OF STATES WERE OPPOSED TO ABORTION FOR ANY REASON EXCEPT TO SAVE THE LIFE OF THE MOTHER.

I'm getting an ultrasound today. Which is my best side?

©2001

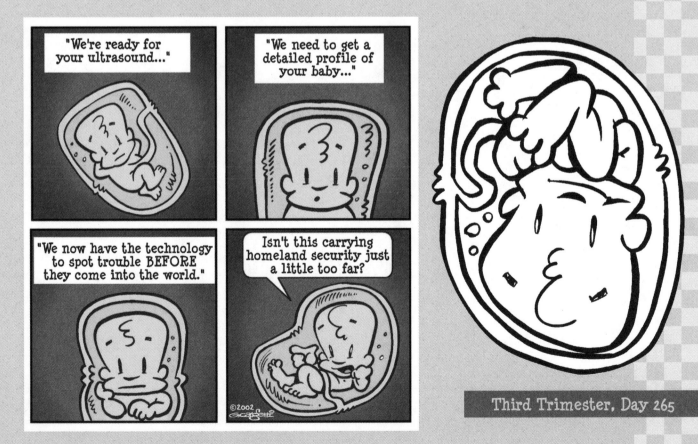

"We're ready for your ultrasound..."

"We need to get a detailed profile of your baby..."

"We now have the technology to spot trouble BEFORE they come into the world."

Isn't this carrying homeland security just a little too far?

©2002

Third Trimester, Day 265

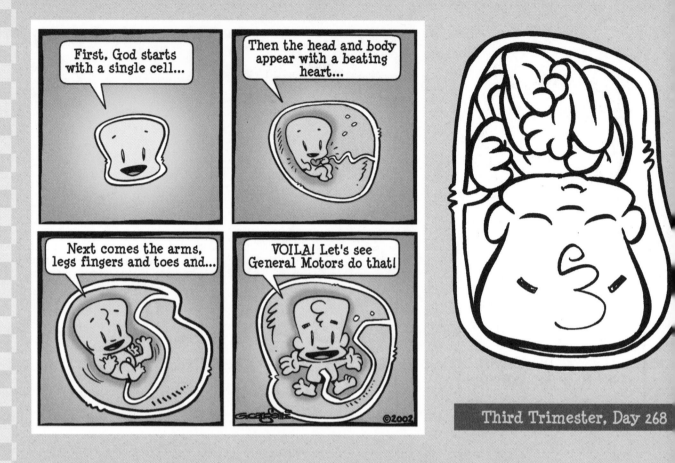

Third Trimester, Day 268

UMBERT'S FACTS OF "LIFE"

IRONICALLY, THE TWO MOST NOTORIOUS SUPREME COURT DECISIONS, ROE V. WADE (UPHOLDING ABORTION) AND DRED SCOTT (UPHOLDING SLAVERY), WERE BOTH DECIDED BY A 7-2 MAJORITY.

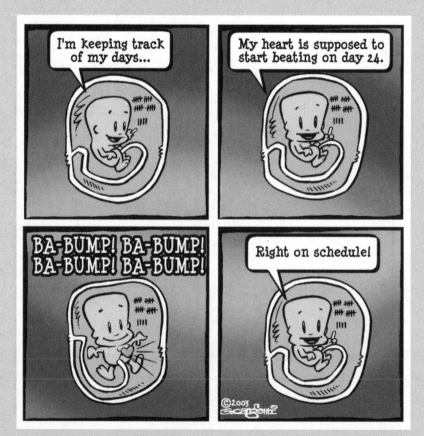

UMBERT'S FACTS OF "LIFE"

UMBERT'S EXTRA "PARTS," THE AMNIOTIC SAC, THE PLACENTA AND THE UMBILICAL CORD, ARE NOT PART OF HIS MOTHER, RATHER, THEY ALL GREW FROM HIS ORIGINAL SINGLE CELL.

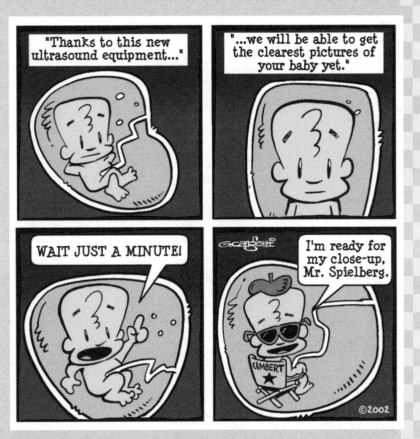

"Thanks to this new ultrasound equipment..."

"...we will be able to get the clearest pictures of your baby yet."

WAIT JUST A MINUTE!

I'm ready for my close-up, Mr. Spielberg.

UMBERT

©2002

To kick or not to kick, that is the question...

Four score and seven days ago, my parents brought forth a new life...

Free at last, free at last, next month I'll be free at last!

I wonder what kind of greatness I'm destined for...

©2002

Third Trimester, Day 270

My heavenly Father, for granting me the gift of creativity and a subject worthy of it.

My parents, John and Ethel (Woodell) Cangemi, whose encouragement nurtured my love for cartooning from an early age.

Helen Gohsler, president, Pennsylvanians for Human Life, whose tireless efforts in defense of the unborn served as the inspiration for "Umbert the Unborn."

Executive Editor Tom Hoopes and the dedicated staff of the *National Catholic Register*, for giving an unknown and an unborn their first big break.

Father Jim Paisley, pastor of St. Maria Goretti Church in Laflin, Pennsylvania, for his support and unwavering belief in Umbert's potential for advancing the pro-life cause.

Most Reverend James C. Timlin, Bishop emeritus of Scranton, Pennsylvania, whose blessing, support, and leadership in the pro-life cause opened doors for Umbert nationwide.

Sue Cirba, education director for Pennsylvanians for Human Life, Scranton Chapter, for her research and editorial contribution for the Umbert's Facts of Life portion of this book.

Dr. Alan H. Firestone, whose friendship and patronage over the years enabled me to pursue worthwhile projects such as "Umbert."

Umbert's REAL parents, the millions of people who have fought and struggled for three decades to overturn the most unjust court ruling in human history and to defend the right of all God's children to take their place among the living.

Umbert's family of publications who gave life to a new approach to the pro-life cause over the past two years:

National Catholic Register
Faith & Family Magazine
The Catholic Light, Scranton, PA
The Catholic Week, Mobile, AL
The Catholic Times, Columbus, OH
New Catholic Miscellany, Charleston, SC
Credo, Ann Arbor, MI
The Catholic Missourian, Jefferson City, MO
Northwest Indiana Catholic, Merrillville, IN
The Tennessee Register, Nashville, TN
Catholic Chronicle, Toledo, OH
West Texas Catholic, Amarillo, TX
Opportunities for Life Hotline News, Frankfort, KY
The Southern Cross, San Diego, CA
North Texas Catholic, Fort Worth, TX
West River Catholic, Rapid City, SD
The Catholic Lighthouse, Victoria, TX
Wyoming Catholic Register, Cheyenne, WY
Knight News, Bartonsville, PA
Cry Out, The Poconos, PA
The Pro-Life Reporter, Scranton, PA
Our Lady of Guadalupe Bulletin, Silvus, IL
St. Thomas Aquinas Bulletin, St. Cloud, FL
And the numerous other pro-life organizations and parishes
who have given "Umbert" a home in their newsletters and bulletins.

Gary Cangemi, 49, was born in Arlington, Virginia and raised in Silver Spring, Maryland, and graduated from Robert E. Peary High School in 1972. A cartoonist from a young age, Gary entertained his classmates and teachers with his drawings and penned comic strips and editorial cartoons for his school newspapers, winning the Award of Excellence from the Maryland High School Journalists Association.

Exploring the possibility of a vocation, he entered St. Pius X Seminary in Dalton, PA and began his studies at the Jesuit-run University of Scranton. He left the seminary after three years and completed his degree in Philosophy in 1976. The following year he became a VISTA volunteer, serving the elderly of the Scranton area and helping to organize the Senior Citizens Advocacy Council. He was hired by Telespond Senior Services to develop senior adult educational programs.

In the late seventies, Cangemi began his career as a freelance editorial cartoonist working with local weeklies and opened the Gary Cangemi Graphic Art Studio in 1982, offering advertising and graphic design services. He also formed a partnership with entrepreneur Larry Newman called CANEW Ideas which licensed several of Cangemi's cartoon concoctions to national companies.

Cangemi continued to focus on local editorial cartooning, working for several different weekly newspapers, lampooning small town politics. A writer as well, he authored the controversial column, The Armchair Commando, a no-holds-barred editorial in which he frequently criticized the abortion industry and the culture of death.

In 2001, seeking a more positive approach to his work, Cangemi launched Umbert the Unborn, an upbeat, pro-life comic strip about a baby in the womb. Now in its third year, Umbert the Unborn is gaining national attention and acclaim by pro-life groups. Cangemi plans to launch an Umbert website and to offer the comic strip for syndication in the mainstream press.

Cangemi continues to reside in Scranton, PA with his wife Nancy, a kindergarten teacher and their three children, Peter, Katherine and Becca where they are members of St. Patrick's Parish. Cangemi has coached youth and high school soccer and was a scoutmaster for ten years. He continues his work as a political cartoonist for the Sunday Voice of Wilkes-Barre and serves on the Board of Directors of Pennsylvanians for Human Life, Scranton Chapter.

Pope John Paul II Cultural Center

Celebrate the legacy of
Pope John Paul II

"...in this dignity
of the human person
...I see the meaning
of history"

3900 Harewood Road, NE
Washington, DC 20017
202-635-5400
www.jp2cc.org
www.popejubilee.org